When was Christ's Death and Resurrection?

Dr. Peter John-Charles

ISBN: 978-1-78364-526-8

www.obt.org.uk

****

The Open Bible Trust
Fordland Mount, Upper Basildon,
Reading, RG8 8LU, UK.

When was Christ's Death and Resurrection?

Contents

Introduction

Introduction

The following is a Biblical attempt to determine the exact chronological date and time on which our Lord Jesus Christ was crucified and when He was resurrected. Attempt is made to find the time; the day of the month; the day of the week; and the year in which these two events took place. (Unless otherwise stated, all quotes are from the *New King James Version* of the Bible). Tradition dictates that Christ died on 'Good Friday' and rose from the dead early on 'Easter' Sunday morning. However is this really what the Bible teaches, and what are the problems with this belief? For one, the original meaning of the word 'Easter' is not a Christian expression. It is the modern form of Eostre, Ostera, Astarte, or Ishtar, the pagan goddess of the rising light of day and spring. Secondly, the long held belief that Jesus died on Easter Friday is based solely on a couple of verses which record that the crucifixion occurred on the day before the Sabbath.

Now when evening had come, because it was the Preparation Day, that is, the day before the Sabbath. (Mark 15:42)

That day was the Preparation, and the Sabbath drew near. Luke 23:54)

However in the Old Testament the word Sabbath (Hebrew, *Shabbath*) had a much wider meaning than just the seventh day of the week. A Sabbath had two key elements: the period of time on which it occurred, namely the seventh; and the presence of rest and cessation of work. With respect to the period of time, the observance of Sabbaths was not restricted to seven periods of days, but was also used to designate seven periods of weeks, years, decades, centuries, or millenaries:

1) Week of Days (Gen: 2-3; Ex 20:11)
2) Week of Weeks (followed by day of Pentecost) (Lev 23:15)
3) Week of Months (Feast months: Abib-Tisri) (Lev 23:4-44)
4) Week of Years (Sabbath year law) (Lev 25:1-5)
5) Week of Week of years (followed by year of Jubilee) Lev 25:8
6) Week of Decades (human life span) (Ps 90:10)
7) Week of Week of decades (Seventy weeks prophecy) (Dan 9:24)
8) Week of Times (7 x 360=2520) (Lev 26:18-28; Lk 21:24)
9) Week of Millenaries (7 x 1000 years)

In addition to the remembrance of the six days of creation, Sabbaths were also associated with feasts and harvests. There were also three kinds of 'rest' that occurred on the Sabbath:

1) a time of rest;
2) no work;
3) no customary work.

*"Remember the **Sabbath** day, to keep it holy. Six days you shall labor and do all your work, but the **seventh day [is] the Sabbath** of the LORD your God. [In it] you shall do **no work**: you, nor your son, nor your daughter, nor your male servant, nor your female servant, nor your cattle, nor your stranger who [is] within your gates. For **[in] six days the LORD made the heavens and the earth, the sea, and all that [is] in them, and rested the seventh day.** Therefore the LORD blessed the **Sabbath** day and hallowed it." (Exodus 20:8-11)*

*"These [are] the **feasts** of the LORD, holy convocations which you shall proclaim at their appointed times. On the **fourteenth [day] of the first month** at twilight [is] the LORD'S **Passover**. And on the **fifteenth day** of the same month [is] the **Feast of Unleavened Bread** to the LORD; **seven days** you must eat unleavened bread. On the **first day** you shall have a holy*

*convocation; you shall do **no customary work** on it. But you shall offer an offering made by fire to the LORD for seven days. The **seventh day** [shall be] a holy convocation; you shall do **no customary work** [on it]." (Leviticus 23:4-8)*

*"And you shall count for yourselves from the day after the Sabbath, from the day that you brought the sheaf of the wave offering: **seven Sabbaths** shall be completed. Count fifty days [i.e. Pentecost] to the day after the **seventh Sabbath**; then you shall offer a new grain offering to the LORD... And you shall proclaim on the same [day] that it is a holy convocation to you. You shall do **no customary work** [on it. it shall be] a statute forever in all your dwellings throughout your generations." (Leviticus 23:15-16, 21)*

*"Also on the day of the firstfruits, when you bring a new grain offering to the LORD at **your [Feast of] Weeks** [i.e. Pentecost], you shall have a holy convocation. You shall do **no customary work**." (Numbers 28:26)*

*Then the LORD spoke to Moses, saying, "Speak to the children of Israel, saying: 'In the **seventh month**, on the **first [day] of the month**, you shall have a **Sabbath-[rest]**. a memorial of **blowing of trumpets**, a holy convocation. You shall do **no customary work** [on it]; and you shall offer an offering made by fire to the LORD.'" (Leviticus 23:23-25)*

*"Also the **tenth [day]** of this **seventh month** [shall be] the **Day of Atonement**. It shall be a holy convocation for you; you shall afflict your souls, and offer an offering made by fire to the LORD. And you shall do **no work** on that same day, for it [is] the **Day of Atonement**, to make atonement for you before the LORD your God... And any person who does any work on that same day, that person I will destroy from among his people. You*

*shall do **no manner of work**; [it shall be] a statute forever throughout your generations in all your dwellings. It [shall be] to you a **sabbath of [solemn] rest**, and you shall afflict your souls; on the ninth [day] of the month at evening, from evening to evening, you shall celebrate your **sabbath**." (Leviticus 23:27-32)*

*"[This] shall be a statute forever for you: In the **seventh month**, on the **tenth [day]** of the month, you shall afflict your souls, and do **no work** at all, [whether] a native of your own country or a stranger who dwells among you." (Leviticus 16:29)*

*"Speak to the children of Israel, saying: 'The **fifteenth day** of this **seventh month**[shall be] the **Feast of Tabernacles** [for] **seven days** to the LORD. On the **first day** [there shall be] a holy convocation. You shall do **no customary work** [on it. For] seven days you shall offer an offering made by fire to the LORD. On the **eighth day** you shall have a holy convocation, and you shall offer an offering made by fire to the LORD. It is a sacred assembly, and you shall do **no customary work** on it.'" (Leviticus 23:34-36)*

*"Six years you shall sow your field, and six years you shall prune your vineyard, and gather its fruit; but in the **seventh year** there shall be a **sabbath** of solemn **rest** for the land, a **sabbath** to the LORD. You shall neither sow your field nor prune your vineyard." (Leviticus 25:3-4)*

Appreciation of the broadness of the word Sabbath prevents automatically associating it to the weekly seventh day. Indeed, the Bible clearly states that the crucifixion took place on the "Preparation Day of the Passover"; and in reference to the Sabbath on the day after the crucifixion, it further records "that Sabbath was a high day".

*Now it was the **Preparation Day of the Passover**, and about the sixth hour. And he (i.e. Pontius Pilate) said to the Jews, "Behold your King!" (John 19:14)*

*Therefore, because it was the **Preparation [Day]**, that the bodies should not remain on the cross on the Sabbath (for **that Sabbath was a high day**), the Jews asked Pilate that their legs might be broken, and [that] they might be taken away. (John 19:31)*

The inclusion of the phrases the "Preparation day of the Passover" and "that Sabbath was a high day" (John 19:14, 31) was used to emphasise and qualify the Sabbath. The day following the crucifixion was not a 'normal' weekly Sabbath. It was the Passover 'high day", i.e. the annual Passover Sabbath. In the section "The date of the month" we shall show that the Passover Sabbath referred to the feast of unleavened bread.

Now the Feast of Unleavened Bread drew near, which is called Passover. (Luke 22:1)

It is the understanding of the Passover as directed in Exodus, Leviticus, Numbers and Deuteronomy and not the mere use of the word 'Easter', which provides the main key in this study. Only by establishing the correct course and timing of the events of the crucifixion and resurrection do we see how perfectly our gracious Lord filled them fully, and indeed why He had to be born under the Law. In our present day the church is predominantly Gentile, but our 'Christian' heritage is a Jewish one. Our substitution of the word 'Passover' with 'Easter', and the fact that 'Good Friday' does not occur on the same date when Jews celebrate their Passover, prevents many believers from realising or acknowledging our heritage.

The time of day

The time of day

Before we discuss the time of the crucifixion and resurrection, it is necessary that we first define some points of time reckoning.

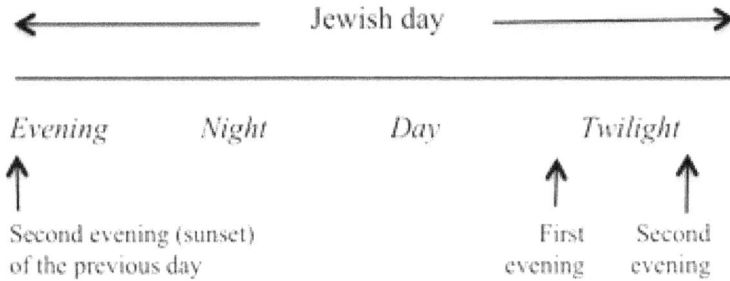

a) The Jewish day is from evening to evening. It is generally believed that this method of reckoning a Jewish day was originally based on the fact that in the 'week of creation', each day began with darkness in the Evening, followed by light in the Morning.

> Then God said, "Let there **be lights in the firmament** of the heavens **to divide the day from the night**; and let them be for signs and seasons, and for days and years; (Genesis 1:14)

> So the **evening and the morning** were the fourth day. (Genesis 1:19)

b) Evening time refers to the period following sunset, and is at the *beginning* of a Jewish day. In the spring season, nighttime is from about 6 pm-6 am, and daytime is from about 6 am-6 pm.

c) The terms 'between the evenings' sometimes translated 'twilight', refer to the period of time at the *end* of a Jewish day as the sun is setting, until sunset.

> *"Now this [is] what you shall offer on the altar: two lambs of the first year, day by day continually. One lamb you shall offer in the morning, and the other lamb you shall offer at **twilight.** [Lit. between the evenings]. (Exodus 29:38-39)*

The 'first evening' is the period when the sun is verging towards setting, and the 'second evening' is the moment of actual sunset. Realising that there are two evenings in each Jewish day is an important key in determining the time of day when some Biblical events occurred. When evening refers to the 'first evening' then it marks the start of the twilight period; and when it refers to the 'second evening', i.e. sunset, it marks the end of one Jewish calendar day, and the beginning of the next Jewish calendar day.

d) The first day of the week was Saturday evening-Sunday evening:

By Gentile reckoning each day of the week begins at midnight, and the 'first day of the week' covers the period from early morning Sunday through to Sunday midnight. However 'days' in the Bible began 6 hours earlier at evening (i.e. 6 pm), so the 'first day of the week' by Jewish reckoning covered six hours of our Saturday evening as well as early morning Sunday through to Sunday evening. Because of that any Scriptural reference to the first day of the week (or weeks) should be carefully studied to determine which day is indicated, either Saturday or Sunday.

e) Some of the Jewish Feast day periods were longer than 24 hours, and involved a part of two Jewish days.

*"Also the **tenth [day] of this seventh month shall be the Day of Atonement**. It shall be a holy convocation for you; you shall afflict your souls, and offer an offering made by fire to the Lord. And you shall do no work on that same day, for it is the Day of Atonement, to make atonement for you before the Lord your God. (Leviticus 23:27-28)*

*It [shall be] to you a sabbath of [solemn] rest, and you shall afflict your souls; **on the ninth [day] of the month at evening, from evening to evening**, you shall celebrate your sabbath."*
(Leviticus 23:32)

Cross reference of Leviticus 23:27-28 with Leviticus 23:32, reveals that the Day of Atonement was on the 10th day of the seventh month (i.e. Tisri), but that it began on the evening of the 9th day. In reference to the Day of Atonement, it would make no sense to make mention of the evening of the 9th day, if the evening meant the 'second evening', since in that case it would involve no part of the 9th day, but rather the start of the 10th day. Hence the evening of the 9th day must refer to the 'first evening' as the sun is verging towards setting. Hence the Day of Atonement was from twilight at the end of the 9th Tisri, and covered the nighttime and daytime periods of the 10th Tisri through to the evening at the end of the 10th Tisri.

Some who hold to a 'Good Friday' crucifixion and 'Easter Sunday' resurrection, point out that sometimes an expression like 'the third day' can include only parts of days, where a part of a day is counted as a whole. Hence when Jesus said "the third day He will rise again", they count part of Friday as one day, Saturday as the second day, and part of Sunday as the third day. There is some Biblical justification for counting part of a day as a whole day. For instance, in Luke 13:32-33 Jesus said, "Behold, I cast out demons and perform cures today and tomorrow, and the third [day] I shall be perfected." Even though only parts of those days are involved, 'the third day', in this case, meant 'the day after tomorrow'.

*And He said to them, "Go, tell that fox, 'Behold, I cast out demons and perform cures today and tomorrow, and **the third [day] I shall be perfected.'** Nevertheless I must journey today, tomorrow, and **the [day] following**; for it cannot be that a prophet should perish outside of Jerusalem. (Luke 13:32-33)*

However, Jesus did not only speak in terms of rising "the third day".

*...and they will mock Him, and scourge Him, and spit on Him, and kill Him. **And the third day He will rise again**. (Mark 10:34)*

*From that time Jesus began to show to his disciples that He must go to Jerusalem, and suffer many things from the elders and chief priests and scribes, and be killed, and **be raised the third day**. (Matthew 16:21)*

He also spoke of this time period, as a specific sign of His Messiahship, as being "three days and three nights" in the heart of the earth.

*But He answered and said to them, "An evil and adulterous generation seeks after a sign, and no sign will be given to it except the sign of the prophet Jonah. For as Jonah was three days and three nights in the belly of the great fish, **so will the Son of Man be three days and three nights in the heart of the earth**." (Matthew 12:39-40)*

At the very least the above verse makes it clear that Jesus was buried for a time period that involved parts of three days and parts of three nights. The latter – namely three nights – is most significant, even in the case of only parts of nights. For instance, had Jesus been buried on Friday, then the earliest time of the resurrection would have been Sunday night, i.e. Friday (Night 1), Saturday (Night 2), and Sunday (Night 3). Hence this verse alone is sufficient to *disprove* a Sunday morning resurrection time. We contend however that the phrase three days and three nights was used to indicate three whole days and three whole nights. By considering a solar day of twelve hours daylight and twelve hours night, this can be represented in terms of hours. The condition of day and night of equal length occurs exactly twice yearly: the vernal equinox on the 21st March, and the autumnal equinox on the 23rd September. (See below)

Annual Daytime hours

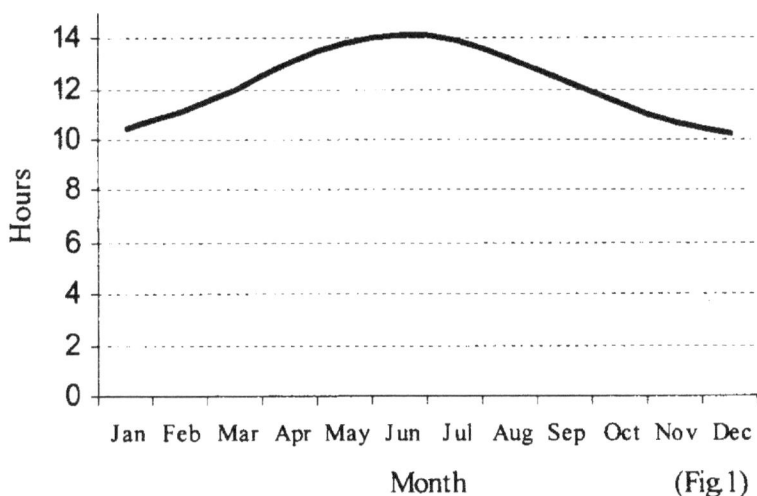

(Fig 1)

*Jesus answered, "Are there not **twelve hours in the day**? If anyone walks in the day, he does not stumble, because he sees the light of this world. But if one walks in the night, he stumbles, because the light is not in him." (John 11:9-10)*

Hence if we figure a full 'three days and three nights', that would equal 72 hours. Jesus was to be in the tomb for 'three days and three nights', and after three days rise again".

> *And He began to teach them that the Son of Man must suffer many things, and be rejected by the elders and chief priests and scribes, and be killed, and **after three days rise again**. (Mark 8:31)*

This indicates at least 72 hours. On the other hand, if He was to be raised from the dead "in three days", this could not be *more* than 72 hours.

> *Jesus answered and said to them, "Destroy this temple, and **in three days I will raise it up**" ... But He was speaking of the temple of His body. Therefore, when He has risen from the dead, His disciples remembered that He had said this to them...(John 2:19, 21-22)*

To harmonise these various time statements (namely "three days and three nights"; "after three days", i.e. ≥ 3 days; and "in three days", i.e. $\leq$ days),it seems reasonable to assume that the time period was 72 hours. Jesus could not have been buried late on Friday afternoon and rose on Sunday early morning, since the time span involved in that case would only

be Friday (Night 1) $\longrightarrow$ Saturday (Day 1 and Night 2),

i.e. one day and two nights (about $3 \times 12 = 36$ hours). That is only half of the time in which Jesus is said to have been in the tomb! Now Jesus died about the 9th hour of the Jewish daytime, i.e. 3 o'clock in the afternoon.

> And **about the ninth hour Jesus cried out** with a loud voice, saying, "Eli, Eli, lama sabachthani?" *that is, "My God, My God, why have you forsaken Me?" Some of those who stood there,*

when they heard [that], said "This Man is calling for Elijah!"
Immediately one of them ran and took a sponge, filled [it] with
sour wine and put [it] on a reed, and offered it to Him to drink.
The rest said, "Let Him alone; let us see if Elijah will come to
*save Him." And **Jesus cried out again with a loud voice, and***
***yielded up His spirit.** (Matthew 27:46-50)*

And the timing of Christ's burial was as follows:

1) After the (first) evening, during the late afternoon twilight
period.

*Now **when evening had come,** there came a rich man from*
Arimathea, named Joseph, who himself had also become a
disciple of Jesus. This man went to Pilate and asked for the body
of Jesus. Then Pilate commanded the body to be given to him.
*When **Joseph had taken the body, he wrapped it in a clean***
linen cloth, and laid it in his new tomb which he had hewn out
***of the rock;** and he rolled a large stone against the door of the*
tomb, and departed. (Matthew 27:57-60)

*Now **when evening had come, because it was the Preparation***
***Day, that is, the day before the Sabbath**, Joseph of Arimathea,*
a prominent council member, who was himself waiting for the
kingdom of God, coming and taking courage, went in to Pilate
and asked for the body of Jesus. Pilate marveled that He was
already dead; and summoning the centurion, he asked him if He
had been dead for some time. And when he found out from the
centurion, he granted to the body to Joseph. Then He bought
fine linen, took Him down, and wrapped Him in the linen. And
***he laid Him in a tomb which had been hewn out of the rock**,*
and rolled a stone against the door of the tomb. (Mark 15:42-
46)

2) Just before sunset at the end of the "Preparation Day of the Passover".

> Now **it was the Preparation Day of the Passover...**And he (i.e. Pilate) said to the Jews, "Behold your King!" ...After this, Joseph of Arimathea, being a disciple of Jesus, but secretly, for fear of the Jews, asked Pilate that he might take away the body of Jesus; and Pilate gave [him] permission. So he came and took the body of Jesus. And Nicodemus, who at first came to Jesus by night, also came, bringing a mixture of myrrh and aloes, about a hundred pounds. Then they took the body of Jesus, and bound it in strips of linen with the spices, as the custom of the Jews is to bury. Now in the place where He was crucified there was a garden, and in the garden a new tomb in which no one had yet been laid. So there **they laid Jesus, because of the Jews' Preparation [Day]**, for the tomb was nearby. (John 19:14, 38-42)

3) As the Passover "Sabbath drew near".

> Now behold, [there was] a man named Joseph, a council member, a good and just man. He had not consented to their decision and deed. [He was] from Arimathea, a city of the Jews, who himself was also waiting for the kingdom of God. This man went to Pilate and asked for the body of Jesus. Then he took it down, wrapped it in linen, and laid it in a tomb [that was] hewn out of the rock, where no one had ever lain before. **That day was the Preparation, and the Sabbath drew near.** (Luke 23:50-54)

Hence applying the literal rendering that Jesus spent exactly three days and three nights in the tomb, to the fact that He was buried at about 6 pm leads to the following conclusion: Jesus rose from the dead three days after His crucifixion at the exact same time of His burial. That is, Jesus rose from the dead at about 6 pm, at the late afternoon sunset, and not at 6 am at the early morning sunrise.

The date
of the month

The date of the month

Jesus was crucified at the time of the yearly Passover, which occurs in the Jewish month Abib, also called Nisan.

*You know that after two days is the **Passover**, and the Son of Man will be delivered up to be **crucified**. (Matthew 26:2)*

***Observe the month of Abib, and keep the Passover** to the LORD your God brought you out of Egypt by night. Therefore you shall sacrifice the Passover to the LORD your God, from the flock and the herd, in the place where the LORD chooses to put His name...but at the place where the LORD your God chooses to make His name abide, there you shall **sacrifice the Passover at twilight, at the going down of the sun,** at the time you came out of Egypt. (Deuteronomy 16:1-2, 6)*

Passover was an annual festival of the Jews. It was kept in remembrance of the Lord's passing over the houses of the Israelites when the firstborn of all the Egyptians were destroyed. It marked one of the most momentous acts of divine intervention in their history, their deliverance from bondage in Egypt.

*Now the LORD spoke to Moses and Aaron in the land of Egypt, saying, "this month (i.e. Abib) [shall be] your beginning of months; it [shall be] the first month of the year to you. Speak to all the congregation of Israel, saying: '**On the tenth [day] of this month every man shall take for himself a lamb**, according to the house of [his] father, a lamb for a household'... Now you shall **keep it until the fourteenth day** of the same month. Then* *the whole assembly of the congregation of Israel shall **kill it at twilight**. And they shall take [some] of the blood and put [it] on the two doorposts and on the lintel of the houses where they eat it... It [is] the LORD'S Passover. For I will pass through the land of Egypt on that night, and will strike all the firstborn in the land of Egypt, both man and beast; and against all the gods of Egypt I will execute judgment: I [am] the LORD. Now the blood shall be a sign for you on the houses where you [are]. And when I see the blood, I will **pass over** you; and the plague shall not be on you to destroy [you] when I strike the land of Egypt. (Exodus 12:1-3, 6-7, 11-13)*

Thus the Passover lamb was *killed* at twilight at the *end* of the 14th Abib. It was then roasted and *eaten* during the next few hours on the night at the *start* of the 15th Abib.

*Then they shall **eat the flesh on that night**; roasted in fire, with unleavened bread [and] they shall eat it. Do not eat it raw, nor boiled at all with water, but roasted in fire-its head with its legs and its entrails. You shall **let none of it remain until morning**, and what remains of it until morning you shall burn with fire. (Exodus 12:8-10)*

Hence the date of the annual Passover, when it referred to the *killing* of the Passover lamb, was the 14th Abib.

*On the **fourteenth [day]** of the first month at twilight **[is] the LORD'S Passover.** (Leviticus 23:5)*

*Now the LORD spoke to Moses in the Wilderness of Sinai, in the first month of the second year after they had come out of the land of Egypt, saying: "Let the children of Israel keep the Passover at its appointed time. **On the fourteenth day of this month, at twilight, you shall keep it at its appointed time.***

*According to all its rites and ceremonies you shall keep it." So Moses told the children of Israel that they should keep the Passover. And **they kept the Passover on the fourteenth day of the first month, at twilight**, in the Wilderness of Sinai; according to all that the LORD commanded Moses so the children of Israel did. (Numbers 9:1-5)*

Passover was followed by "the Feast of Unleavened Bread" on the 15th Abib. It began a period of "seven days" on which the Israelites were instructed "to eat unleavened bread". On "the first day" all the Israelites gathered together, holy convocation, and did "no customary work on it" (Leviticus 23:7). Hence the first day of eating unleavened bread was a Sabbath day, since Sabbath means 'to rest from labour'.

*And on the **fifteenth day of the same month [is] the Feast of Unleavened Bread** to the LORD; seven days you must eat unleavened bread. On the first day you shall have a holy convocation; **you shall do no customary work on it.** (Leviticus 23:6-7)*

In the Old Testament, the word 'Passover' usually referred to the *killing* of the Passover lamb on the 14th Abib at twilight. However in the New Testament at the time of our Lord, 'Passover' was more commonly used in reference to the 'Feast of Unleavened Bread' on the 15th Abib, when the Passover lamb was *eaten*. In the Scriptures the inclusion of the word "Feast", is used to reference the Passover Sabbath day of the Feast of Unleavened Bread on the 15th Abib.

*You shall not offer the blood of My sacrifice with leaven, nor shall the sacrifice of the **Feast of the Passover** be left until morning. (Exodus 34:25)*

*Now the **Feast of Unleavened Bread** drew near, which is **called Passover**. (Luke 22:1)*

*Now before the **feast of the Passover**, when Jesus knew that His hour had come that He should depart from this world to the Father, having loved His own who were in the world, He loved them to the end. (John 13:1)*

This change in emphasis concerning the Passover was symptomatic of increasing secularism within the nation of Israel. They placed more importance on the feasting and eating of the Passover lamb, than they did on the religious aspect of its sacrifice. Exodus 12:18 provides another important key to correctly determining the date of the annual Passover Sabbath day, i.e. the Feast day of Unleavened bread. In the previous section (part e), we saw that the Day of Atonement on the 10th Tisri began from the twilight period on the 9th Tisri. In like manner, the Feast of Unleavened Bread on the 15th Abib, began from the 'first evening', i.e. the twilight period on the 14th Abib.

And on the fifteenth day of this month [is] the feast; unleavened bread shall be eaten for seven days. (Numbers 28:17)

In the first month, on the fourteenth day of the month at evening, you shall eat unleavened bread, until the twenty-first day of the month at evening. (Exodus 12:18)

Hence the first day of eating unleavened bread was from the twilight period approaching the end of the 14th Abib to the evening at the end of the 15th Abib. Because the first day of eating unleavened bread involved part of the 14th Abib and all of the 15th Abib, the dates of the "first day" were as follows:

*Seven days you shall eat unleavened bread. On the **first day** (14th Abib) you shall remove leaven from your houses. For whoever eats leavened bread from the **first day** (twilight 14th Abib to end of 15th Abib) until the seventh day (21st Abib), that person shall be cut off from Israel. On the **first day** (twilight 14th Abib to end of 15 Abib) there shall be a holy convocation, and on the seventh day (21st Abib) there shall be a holy convocation for you...(Exodus 12:15-16)*

Hence there are two 'first days', the 14th and 15th Abib. The 'Day of Unleavened Bread' (Luke 22:7) or 'first day of Unleavened Bread' (Mark 14:12; Matthew 26:17), refers to all of the 14th Abib, and involves the *removing* of leaven from Jewish houses, and the killing of the Passover lamb at the end of the 14th Abib at twilight. Whereas, the 'first day' of *eating* unleavened bread refers to the Feast of Unleavened Bread, i.e. the Passover Sabbath 'high day', and is from twilight at the end of 14th Abib to the evening at the end of the 15th Abib.

*Then came the **Day of Unleavened Bread**, when the Passover must be killed. (Luke 22:7)*

*Now on the **first day of Unleavened Bread, when they killed the Passover** [lamb], His disciples said to Him, "Where do you want us to go and prepare, that You may eat the Passover?" (Mark 14:12)*

*Now on the **first** [day] **of the [Feast of] Unleavened Bread** the disciples came to Jesus, saying to Him, "Where do You want us to prepare for You to eat the Passover?" (Matthew 26:17)*

In the Scriptures, words that are in italics were not in the original text. (In our Scripture references, we have used brackets instead of italics). The inclusion of the word "*Feast*" in Matthew 26:17 above is incorrect. The word is correctly omitted in the corresponding verses Luke 22:7 and Mark 14:12, since the day and time in question was the beginning of the calendar day 14th Abib, and not at the end of the 14 Abib at twilight.

The events of the 14th-21st Abib were as follows:

- **14th Abib:** The 'first day of Unleavened Bread' when leaven was removed from the houses (Exodus 12:15b, Deuteronomy 16:4b); the Passover lamb was killed at the end of that day at twilight (Exodus 12:6, Leviticus 23:5, Numbers 28:16, Deuteronomy 16:6).

- **Twilight 14 Abib-15th Abib:** The Feast of Unleavened Bread, the 'first day' of eating unleavened bread (Exodus 12:14, 17, Leviticus 23:6a, Numbers 28:17a); there was a holy gathering (Exodus 12:16a, Leviticus 23:7a, Numbers 28:18a); it was a Sabbath day (Exodus 12:16c, Leviticus 23:7b, Numbers 28:18b); in the night (at the start of 15th Abib) the Passover lamb was eaten (Exodus 12:8-10).

- **15th-21st Abib:** Eat unleavened bread (Exodus 12:15a, c, 18-20, Leviticus 23:6b, Numbers 28:17b, Deuteronomy 16:3-4a); and offering by fire (Leviticus 23:8a, Numbers 28:19-24).

- **21st Abib:** There was a holy gathering (Exodus 12:16b, Leviticus 23:8b, Numbers 28:25a, Deuteronomy 16:8); it was a Sabbath day (Exodus 12:16c, Leviticus 23:8c, Numbers 28:25b).

Hence, the immediate days surrounding Christ's crucifixion included an annual Passover Sabbath (the Feast of Unleavened Bread), from twilight at the end of the 14th Abib to the evening at the end of 15th Abib; as well as the usual weekly Sabbaths. It thus becomes clear that the 'high day' Sabbath referred to in John 19:31 was this annual Passover Sabbath, and not the weekly Sabbath.

Much of the confusion concerning the dating of Christ's death and resurrection, has occurred because this 'high day' Sabbath has been mistaken for the 'weekly' Sabbath. John 19:14 makes it clear that Jesus was crucified on the "Preparation Day of the Passover". Now 'Preparation Day' is "the day before the Sabbath" (Mark 15:42). Hence it was the Preparation Day of the Passover Sabbath, i.e. the day before the Passover Sabbath. As we have seen above the Passover Sabbath was on the 15th Abib, and referred to the Feast of Unleavened Bread. So the "Preparation Day of the Passover" was in fact the Preparation Day of the Feast of Unleavened Bread, i.e. the day before the Feast of Unleavened Bread. We are now able to ascertain the *date of the month* of Christ's death and resurrection. Jesus died in the afternoon of the 14th Abib, the calendar day before the Feast of Unleavened Bread called Passover (Luke 22:1; John 19:14, 31). He was buried later that day at sunset. Travelling forward in time "three days and three nights", reveals the date and time of the resurrection, as the end of the 17th Abib at sunset. (This will be further confirmed and substantiated in the following section).

The day
of the week

The day of the week

We begin our investigation to find the *day of the week* when Christ was resurrected by highlighting a recurrent mistranslation in the Biblical narrative.

*Now after the Sabbath, as the **first [day] of the week** began to dawn, Mary Magdalene and the other Mary came to see the tomb. (Matthew 28:1)*

*Very early in the morning, on the **first [day] of the week**, they came to the tomb when the sun had risen. (Mark 16:2)*

*Now when [He] rose early on the **first [day] of the week**, he appeared first to Mary Magdalene, out of whom He had cast seven demons. (Mark 16:9)*

*Now on the **first [day] of the week**, very early in the morning, they, and certain [other women] with them, came to the tomb bringing the spices which they had prepared. (Luke 24:1)*

*On the **first [day] of the week** Mary Magdalene went to the tomb early, while it was still dark, and saw [that] the stone had been taken away from the tomb. (John 20:1)*

The above verses all include the words: *...the first [day] of the week...*

However there are two errors in this short excerpt.
1) The word 'day' is not in the original text;

2) According to *Young's Literal Translation of the Bible,* an 's' has been omitted from the word 'week', so these verses should read: *...the first of the weeks (or Sabbaths)...*

The significance of this omission is failure to see that the true meaning is not merely the first day of the week (i.e. Saturday evening-Sunday evening), but the first day of a 49 day period known as the 'seven weeks' or 'seven Sabbaths'. The day following the seven weeks, i.e. The 50th day (or Pentecost), was the Feast of Weeks.

> ***Count fifty days*** *(i.e. Pentecost)* ***to the day after the seventh Sabbath****; then you shall offer a new grain offering to the LORD...And you shall proclaim on the same day [that]* ***it is a holy convocation to you.*** *You shall do no customary work [on it. It shall be] a statute forever in all your dwellings throughout your generations. (Leviticus 23:16,21)*

> *Then you shall keep the* ***Feast of Weeks*** *(i.e. Pentecost) to the LORD your God with the tribute of a freewill offering from your hand, which you shall give as the LORD your God blesses you (Deuteronomy 16:10)*

> *Now when the* ***Day of Pentecost*** *had fully come, they were all with one accord in one place. (Acts 2:1)*

Pentecost was the 50th day of the weeks. However, for there to have been a 50th day, there also had to be a first day of the weeks! With this correction in mind (plural weeks or Sabbaths), it becomes relevant to ascertain which day of the week was the first day of the seven weeks/Sabbaths. Now the 'seven Sabbaths' start from the day of the sheaf wave offering, on the day after the Sabbath.

*He (the priest) shall wave the sheaf before the LORD, to be accepted on your behalf; on **the day after the Sabbath** the priest shall wave it. (Leviticus 23:11)*

*And you shall count for yourselves from **the day after the Sabbath**, from the day that you brought the sheaf of the wave offering: seven Sabbaths shall be completed. (Leviticus 23:15)*

In Israel, the feasts to the Lord coincided with their harvest times. For instance, the 'seven weeks' between the Passover and Pentecost coincided with the time of harvesting the barley crop.

You shall count seven weeks for yourself; begin to count the seven weeks from [the time] you begin [to put] the sickle to the grain. (Deuteronomy 16:9)

*Speak to the children of Israel, and say to them: "When you come into the land which I give to you, **and reap its harvest, then you shall bring a sheaf of the firstfruits of your harvest to the priest."** (Leviticus 23:10)*

Here too however, there was contention concerning the Sabbath which marked the day before the waving of the sheaf of firstfruits and the beginning of the 'seven weeks' of harvesting. Because instruction for the sheaf wave offering was preceded by instruction for both the keeping of the weekly Sabbath (Leviticus 23:3), and the Passover Sabbath (Leviticus 23:5-7), there arose contention between the Pharisees and the Sadducees concerning whether the Sabbath in question was the *Passover* Sabbath on the 15th Abib, or the first *weekly* Sabbath after the Passover Sabbath.

*Six days shall work be done, but **the seventh day [is] a Sabbath of solemn rest**, a holy convocation. **You shall do no work [on it]; it [is] the Sabbath** of the LORD in all your dwellings... On* *the fourteenth [day] of the first month at twilight [is] the LORD"S Passover. And on the fifteenth day of the same month [is] the Feast of Unleavened Bread to the LORD; seven days you must eat unleavened bread.* **On the first day you shall have a holy convocation; you shall do no customary work on it** *(i.e. a Sabbath). (Leviticus 23:3, 5-7)*

At the time of the second Temple, the Pharisees counted the seven weeks as commencing from the day after the *Passover* Sabbath. Hence the day of the sheaf wave offering would always be the 16th Abib, and the fiftieth day (Pentecost) would always be the 6th Sivan. On the other hand, the Sadducees counted the seven weeks as commencing from the day after the first *weekly* Sabbath following the Passover Feast. Now, by Jewish reckoning the weekly Sabbath is the last day of the week, so the day after the weekly Sabbath corresponds to the first day of the week, i.e. the 'first day of the seven weeks' was the same as the 'first day of the week'! Thus the Sadducees reckoned the 'first of the weeks' as the first Saturday evening to Sunday evening, after the Passover Sabbath on the 15th Abib. Hence the day of the sheaf wave offering would always be a Saturday evening-Sunday evening,, and Pentecost would also always be a Saturday evening-Sunday evening (see the section 'The days of the seven Sabbaths/weeks' for a chart of those days). Thus the Pharisees reckoned the start of the seven weeks and Pentecost fifty days later, in terms of *calendar dates,* i.e. 16th Abib to 6th Sivan respectively, whereas the Sadducees reckoned the start of the seven weeks and Pentecost, in terms of the *days of the week,* both events occurring on a Saturday evening-Sunday evening. The day of the week of 'the first of the Sabbaths', at the time of our Lord is thus related to who were the dominant religious leaders at that time: the Sadducees or the Pharisees? Scripture provides the answer to this question, and informs us that Caiaphas of the sect of the Sadducees was the high priest at that time (27-36 AD).

When was Christ's Death and Resurrection?

*Then the chief priests, the scribes, and the elders of the people assembled at the palace of **the high priest, who was called Caiaphas**. (Matthew 26:3)*

*Then the **high priest** rose up, and all those who [were] with him **(which is the sect of the Sadducees)**, and they were filled with indignation. (Acts 5:17)*

Caiaphas and the Sadducees, were in leadership of the Sanhedrin (the religious council) and their power was localized in Jerusalem. They attributed great religious significance to the sacrificial worship of the temple (and with few interruptions they remained in control of the Sanhedrin until the destruction of Jerusalem in 70 AD). Hence they would have ensured that the 'first day of the weeks' would have occurred on the correct day, i.e. the first Saturday evening-Sunday evening, after the Passover Sabbath on the 15 Abib. Now even in respect to the first day of the seven-day week, there is no scriptural precedent that the phrase "first day of the week" referred merely to our Sunday. As stated earlier, it also included the preceding last six hours of Saturday.

On the first [day] of the week let each one of you lay something aside, storing up as he may prosper, that there be no collections when I come. (1 Corinthians 16:2)

*Now **on the first [day] of the week**, when the disciples came together to break bread, Paul, ready to depart the next day, spoke to them and **continued his message until midnight**. (Acts 20:7)*

In the latter case Paul began speaking to the disciples on the first day of the week "and continued his message until midnight". Hence he evidently began speaking to the disciples on Saturday evening. Now the women and the disciples who visited the tomb on the first of the Sabbaths, on Saturday evening and on Sunday morning, found an empty tomb, because Jesus had already risen by then.

Now **after the Sabbath, as the first [day] of the week began to dawn,** (i.e. early Saturday evening) *Mary Magdalene and the other Mary came to see the tomb. And behold, there was a great earthquake; for an angel of the Lord descended from heaven, and came and rolled back the stone from the door, and sat on it. (Matthew 28:1-2)*

Now **when [He] rose early on the first [day] of the week,** (i.e. *Saturday evening), He appeared first to Mary Magdalene...(Mark 16:9)*

Now **on the first [day] of the week** *Mary Magdalene went to the tomb early, while it was still dark, (i.e. Saturday evening) and* **saw [that] the stone had been taken away from the tomb.** *Then she ran and came to Simon Peter, and to the other disciple, whom Jesus loved, and said to them, "**They have taken away the Lord out of the tomb,** and we do not know where they have laid Him." (John 20:1-2)*

Now **on the first [day] of the week, very early in the morning** *(i.e. Sunday morning), they, and certain [other women] with them, came to the tomb bringing the spices which they had prepared. But **they found the stone rolled away from the tomb.** Then they went in and **did not find the body of the Lord Jesus.** And it happened, as they were greatly perplexed about this, that behold, two men stood by them in shining garments. Then, as they were afraid and bowed [their] faces to the earth, they said to them, "Why do you seek the living among the dead? **He is not here, but is risen!** Remember how He spoke to you when He was still in Galilee." (Luke 24:1-6)*

*But the angel answered and said to the women, "Do not be afraid, for I know that you seek Jesus who was crucified. **He is not here; for He is risen**, as He said. Come, see the place where the Lord lay." (Matthew 28:5-6)*

In the Greek there are no punctuation marks, so the placing of the comma after 'week' in Mark 16:9 above, may or may not be correct. However whether the emphasis of 'early on the first day of the week' refers to when Jesus arose or when he appeared to Mary, is immaterial. In either case it would indicate that Jesus rose on Saturday evening. Gentile interpretations that Christ rose between 4 am-6 am on Sunday morning do not fit the phrase 'early on the first day of the week' since in such a scenario by Jewish time the first day of the week would already be 10-12 hours old! If anything else were meant other than evening at the start of the Jewish day, it would have been possible to be more specific.

*Watch therefore, for you do not know when the master of the house is coming-in the **evening** (sunset-bedtime), at **midnight**, at the **crowing of the rooster** (midnight-3 am), or in the **morning** (sunrise-noon) (Mark 13:35)*

The reference to both the end of the Sabbath and the beginning of the weeks in Matthew 28:1, is possibly the clearest indication that the resurrection at the epoch between those two days, namely at 6 pm on Saturday evening. We contend that Matthew 28:1, 'after the Sabbath as the first *day* of the weeks began to dawn' is equivalent to Leviticus 23:15.

*And you shall count for yourselves from the **day after the Sabbath**, from the day that you brought the sheaf of the wave offering: **seven Sabbaths** shall be completed. (Leviticus 23:15*

Hence a much better translation of Matthew 28:1 would have been: *Now late on the Sabbath, at the dawn towards the first [day] of the [seven] weeks…*

The weekly Sabbath had not yet ended when Mary Magdalene and the other Mary (mother of James the Less and Joses, Mark 15:40) were coming to see the tomb. And behold they evidenced the earthquake which probably heralded the resurrection.

> *And behold, **there was a great earthquake**; for an angel of the Lord descended from heaven, and came and **rolled back the stone from the door**, and sat on it. (Matthew 28:2)*

Hence, Jesus rose at the epoch of sunset, at the end of the weekly Sabbath, i.e. on Saturday at about 6 pm, the end of the 17th Abib. Thus His burial which occurred 'three days and three nights' earlier, was on Wednesday at about 6 pm, the end of the 14th Abib.

The year

The year

In the Appendix of my book *Biblical Chronology,* published by The Open Bible Trust, I investigated aspects involved in the chronological dating of the year of the crucifixion, namely the workings of various systems of measuring years: the Julian calendar; the Gregorian calendar; the accuracy of the Gregorian calendar; and backdating the Gregorian calendar. (*Biblical Chronology* was a thorough five-year study that attempted to date every reference to year and month in the Bible. In particular it dated the year of Creation, the years of the patriarchs, the Flood, the Exodus, the reigns of the kings of Judah and Israel, the nativity and crucifixion of Christ, and the Acts of the Apostles).

In the Appendix of *Biblical Chronology* I briefly explain the history of the Jewish lunar calendar and provide astronomical confirmation of the date of the crucifixion. It is however, from scripture, from the prophecy of the 'seventy weeks' in Daniel 9:24-27 which provides the chronological frame for dating the year of the crucifixion. Since the giving of the law and the Ten Commandments to the nation of Israel in 1446 BC, they had repeatedly backslid from the Lord. So 840 years later in 606 BC, the divided kingdom of Judah experienced their first desolation and deportation of their leading men to Babylon at the hand of Nebuchadnezzar. Daniel was taken captive at that time. Then after 68 years into his captivity, in the first year of Darius the Mede, i.e. in 538 BC, he began to understand that the duration of the captivity was soon to end.

In the first year of Darius the son of Ahasuerus of the lineage of
the Medes, who was made king over the realm of the Chaldeans-
in the first year of his reign I, Daniel, understood by the books

*the number of the years [specified] by the word of the LORD through Jeremiah the prophet, that He would accomplish **seventy years** in the **desolations** of Jerusalem. (Daniel 9:1-2)*

*'And this whole land shall be a **desolation** [and] an astonishment, and these nations shall serve the king of Babylon **seventy years.** Then it will come to pass, when **seventy years** are completed, [that] I will punish the king of Babylon and that nation, the land of the Chaldeans, for their iniquity,' says the LORD; 'and I will make it a perpetual desolation.' (Jeremiah 25:11-12)*

*For thus says the LORD: After **seventy years** are completed at Babylon, I will visit you and perform My good word toward you, and **cause you to return to this place.** (Jeremiah 29:10)*

Daniel responded to this new understanding by praying (Jeremiah 29:12-14; Daniel 9:3-19), and the Lord sent the angel Gabriel to him in answer to his prayer (Daniel 9:20-23. Below we present a literal translation (using *Strong's Greek/Hebrew Dictionary*), and include interpretation remarks in parentheses of what Gabriel revealed to him:

*24**Seventy weeks** (Lit. seventy sevens) are determined for your people (Israel) and for your holy city (Jerusalem), to finish the transgression (Daniel 9:5c), and to make an end of sins (Daniel 9:5a), and to atone for iniquity (Daniel 9:5b), and to bring in everlasting righteousness, and to seal up (shut up/close) vision and prophet (all visions and prophecies fulfilled), and to anoint the Most Holy. (the temple, the place of worship)*

*25Know then and understand, from the going forth of the word (decree) to restore and to build Jerusalem (444 BC, Nehemiah 2:1-9) **until Messiah the Prince, seven weeks (Lit. seven sevens), and sixty and two weeks (Lit. Sixty-two sevens);** the* *broad place (market place) and* **rampart (wall) shall be built again, even in the times of narrow bit.** *(the seven weeks)*

[26]*And* **after the sixty and two weeks (Lit. sixty-two sevens), Messiah shall be cut off** *and not is to Him (He shall have nothing). And the city and the sanctuary shall destroy (in 70 AD) the people (Roman army) of a coming prince (a leader yet to come); and its end with the flood (overwhelming army, Daniel 11:22), and until end war are determined desolations.*

[27]*And he (the future leader of Rome) shall confirm a covenant with the many (the majority), one seven (7 years). And in the half of the seven (after 3 ½ years) he shall make cease sacrifice and offering, and upon a wing (pinnacle/peak of the temple), abominations (idols), a desolator even until end (3 ½ years of the great tribulation, Matthew 24:15-22). And that which was decreed shall pour out on the desolator.*

For the sake of this study we limit interpretation of this prophecy to the parts which deal with the 'seventy sevens', i.e. 70 x 7 = 490 (Daniel 9:24). The prophecy did not qualify the 490 in terms of days or years. As we shall show, part of the prophecy was fulfilled in 'days' and part of it was fulfilled in 'years'. Daniel was initially concerned with knowing when the period of the desolations of Jerusalem would come to an end (Daniel 9:2). Jerusalem was in fact desolated three times and captives taken to Babylon:

1) Daniel and others were taken captive in 606 BC in the fourth year of Jehoichim (Jeremiah 25:1-11; 2 Kings 241-4). In Daniel 1:1-7 however it is recorded as the third year. That is because 4 Hebrew reckoned years = accession year + 3 Babylonian reckoned years. The Babylonians used the accession year system, whereby the last year of the old king was not counted for the new king. Daniel wrote the book of Daniel to all Israel. That included his

brethren from the tribes of Judah and Benjamin as well as the much larger number from the ten tribes of Israel who had previously been taken captive in 722 BC. Daniel used Babylonian chronology because it was the most commonly used method of reckoning time during that period of their history.

> *...to the men of **Judah**, to the inhabitants of **Jerusalem** and **all Israel, those near and those far off in all the countries** to which You have driven them... (Daniel 9:7)*

2) Ezekiel was carried captive in 597 BC in the captivity of King Jehoiachin. (Ezekiel 1:2; 2 Kings 24:8-16)

3) King Zedekiah was taken captive and Jerusalem destroyed in 586 BC. (2 Kings 25:1-21; 2 Chronicles 36:15-21)

Daniel was given the prophecy in 538 BC, and he was informed by Gabriel that it was 490 'days' to "finish the transgression, and to make an end of sins, and to atone for iniquity" (Daniel 9:24). This occurred in 536 BC (70 years after the 606 BC captivity, and 490 days after Gabriel had spoken to Daniel), when Cyrus issued a decree liberating the Jewish captives, and permitting them to return to Jerusalem and to rebuild the temple (2 Chronicles 36:22-23; Ezra 1:2). Daniel 9:25 includes two times periods, namely seven weeks (Lit. seven sevens), meaning 7 x 7 = 49 'days' and 'years', and sixty-two weeks (Lit. sixty two sevens), meaning 62 x 7 = 434 'years'. It also defines two events, "until Messiah the Prince" and the rebuilding of the "broad place and rampart (wall)" in Jerusalem. Both events are fixed in time, from the beginning of the seven weeks, "from the going forth of the word (decree) to restore and to build Jerusalem" (Daniel 9:25). The only decree in Scripture authorizing the rebuilding of the city and its wall is recorded in Nehemiah 2:1-9. It occurred "in the month of Nisan (also called Abib, i.e. Mar-Apr), in the twentieth year of King Artaxerxes"

(Nehemiah 2:1). The 1st of Nisan is implied, and this date corresponds to Saturday 4th March 444 BC. (see calendar A1 in the Appendix of (*Biblical Chronology*)

Absolute dates for the reign of King Artaxerxes can be established through knowledge of the dates for the preceding king Xerxes, and the usurper Artabanus. The dates for Xerxes are well known because he conducted invasions of Greece, and Greek historians dated their reigns in terms of the well-understood Olympiad dating system (the repeated four-yearly interval of the Olympic games, which commenced in 776 BC). In addition we have sources from the Ancient Near East, which include papyri from Egypt dated to the reign of Artaxerxes, and tablets of contracts written in cuneiform when Babylonia was under Persian control. We also have Ptolemy's Canon, in which the reigns of ancient kings back to the mid-eighth century BC were dated and fixed by means of eclipses and astronomical-mathematical calculations. We are thus in a very good position to ascertain accurate dates for Xerxes, and for his son Artaxerxes:

1. Classical historical source.

The classical (Greco-Roman) historian Diodorus of Sicily gives us the most precise date for the murder of Xerxes' by Artabanus. It is dated both by the annual election of the chief magistrate in Greece (the Athenian archonship) and the annual election of the chief magistrate in Rome (the Roman consular). These two types of years overlap to indicate that Xerxes was murdered sometime during the last half of the Julian year 465 BC. (See *Diodorus Siculus, 11.69.1-6*)

2. Egyptian-Jewish historical sources.

Papyri from the fifth century BC written in Aramaic by Jewish military mercenaries under Persian conscription on the island of Elephantine in Egypt supply additional historical and chronological information. The Cowley papyrus No. 6 was dated to the twenty-first (and last) year of Xerxes. (See *A. E. Cowley, "Aramaic Papyri of the Fifth Century BC", Oxford University, 1923, p15-18)*. The day and month dates utilized in this document fix its writing to January 2, 464 BC. This text indicates that Xerxes' death had been reported in Egypt by that time. It would have taken a few weeks for delivery of that news in Egypt, indicating that Xerxes died at the very end of 465 BC.

3. Egyptian astronomical source.

Although the Egyptian solar calendar was approximately 0.24220 days short of a true solar year, it advanced regularly in relation to the Julian years used to calculate BC dates. This allows modern historians to convert ancient Egyptian dates into the present day calendar system. The astronomer Ptolemy in his Almagest used this feature. (See *J. Neuffer, "The Accession of Artaxerxes I," Andrews University Seminary Studies 6 (1968): p60-87)*. According to Egyptian reckoning, Xerxes died about the time of the Egyptian New Year's day on 1st Thoth. In the year 465 BC, 1st Thoth corresponded to 17th December. Hence Xerxes died soon after 17th December 465 BC.

The Babylonian 8-year cyclic calendar (See the Appendix-History of the Jewish Lunar calendar) had been made the standard throughout the Persian Empire since the conquest of Babylonia in 539 BC. Publicly, royal years were reckoned in Babylonian style from Nisanu (Nisan) 1. However as a court official, Nehemiah would have known the exact date of Artaxerxes' accession. Thus in the court, the years of a king's reign could be counted more accurately from the accession day (or month). This does appear to have been the case since Nehemiah mentions both Chisleu (November) (Nehemiah 1:1), and the following Nisan (March) (Nehemiah 2:1) in relation to Artaxerxes' twentieth year. Now Xerxes was murdered some time around December 465 BC, and his usurper Artabanus only reigned for seven months. Thus the accession month of Artaxerxes would have been July 464 BC; and the first year of his reign would have been from July 464 BC to July 463 BC. Correspondingly his twentieth year would have been from July 445 BC to July 444 BC. Hence the decree on 1st Nisan, occurred in the year 444 BC, on Saturday 4th March.

The above translation of Daniel 9:25 differs from that of most translations. Usually the verse is concluded "even in times of affliction", however we have translated it as "even in the times of narrow bit". This is taken to mean that the rebuilding of the "broad place and rampart (wall)" takes place after the smaller time period, i.e. in 49 'days' or 'years'. As we shall now demonstrate, the wall was indeed built in 49 days. The command to rebuild Jerusalem was given by Artaxerxes on the 1st Nisan (Saturday 4th March 444 BC). Nehemiah then went to Jerusalem and arrived on the 4th Ab (Monday 3rd July). This date is implied from the fact that the wall was rebuilt on the 25th Elul (Wednesday 23rd August 444 BC), 52 days after his arrival in Jerusalem (Nehemiah 6:15). However the work did not start until he viewed the broken down walls 3 days after his arrival, i.e. on the 7th Ab (Nehemiah 2:11-18). Hence the time rebuilding the wall was the 7th Ab to the 25th Elul. That is 52-3 = 49 days, i.e. seven weeks of days. (Daniel 9:25b)

*And it came to pass in the **month of Nisan**, in the twentieth year of King Artaxerxes (i.e. 444 BC), [when] wine was before him, that I took the wine and gave it to the king... And I said to the* *king, "...I ask that you send me to Judah, to the city of my fathers' tombs, that I may rebuild it." ...**So it pleased the king to send me**; and I set him a time. Furthermore I said to the king, "if it pleases the king, let letters be given to me for the governors [of the region] beyond the River, that they must permit me to pass through till I come to Judah, and a letter to Asaph the keeper of the king's forest, that he must give me timber to make beams for the gates of the citadel which [pertains] to the temple, for the **city wall**, and for the house that I will occupy." And the king **granted** [them] to me according to the good hand of my God upon me. (Nehemiah 2:1, 5-8)*

*So **I came to Jerusalem and was there three days**. Then I arose in the night, I and a few men with me; I told no one what my God had put in my heart to do at Jerusalem; nor was there any animal with me, except the one on which I rode. And I went out by night through the Valley Gate to the Serpent Well and the Refuse Gate, and viewed the walls of Jerusalem which were broken down and its gates which were burned with fire... So I went up in the night by the valley, and viewed the wall; then I turned back and entered by the Valley Gate, and so returned. And the officials did not know where I had gone or what I had done; **I had not yet told the Jews, the priests, the nobles, the officials, or the others who did the work**. Then I said to them, "You see the distress that we [are] in, how Jerusalem [lies] waste, and its gates are burned with fire. Come and let us build the wall of Jerusalem, that we may no longer be a reproach." And I told them of the hand of my God which had been good upon me, and also of **the king's words** that he had spoken to me. So they said, "Let us rise up and build." Then they set their hands to [this] good [work]. (Nehemiah 2:11-18)*

*So the **wall was finished** on the twenty-fifth [day] of Elul, **in fifty-two days**. (Nehemiah 6:15)*

With regards the fulfilment of "until Messiah the Prince", the time interval was in terms of 'years', namely "seven weeks and sixty-two weeks" of years, i.e. 49 + 434 = 483 years. Now a 'year' can mean 354 days (a lunar year) or 384 days (additional month lunar leap year); 360 days (a 'time'), 365 days (a Gregorian year) or 366 days (additional day Gregorian leap year); 365.25 days (a Julian year) or 365.24220 days (an astronomical solar year). Since a single event is prophesied it is needful to know which meaning of 'year' to use. The lengths of the years in this prophecy were in fact 360 days. This is proved by the Biblical references to the 70th week of seven years, which is divided into two halves in Daniel 9:27. The latter 3 ½ years was also defined in terms of 1260 days, 42 months, and 3 ½ 'times', which implies 30-day months and 360-day years.

a) 1260 days (Revelation 11:3; 12:6);
b) forty-two months = 42x30=1260 days (Revelation 11:2;13:5);
c) "a time and times and half a time" =360 + 2x360 + ½x360 = 3½x360 = 1260 days (Daniel 7:25; Revelation 12:14).

A 'time' was an ancient reference to a year which had 360 days. Hence the years of the 'seventy weeks' are all 360 days duration. The moon and the sun are collectively used to measure time, since Genesis 1:14 says "let them be for signs and seasons, and for days and years." Hence it is logical to use 360-day years composed of twelve 30-day months, since these measures of month and year are the arithmetic mean (average) of the lunar (moon) and solar (sun) periods.

	Month (days)	Year (days)
Lunar	29.53059	354.36707
Solar	30.43685	365.24220
Mean	29.98372	359.80463

From 4 March 444 BC it is 7x7 + 62x7 = 483 years "until Messiah the Prince (Daniel 9:25). "And after the sixty and two weeks", i.e. after the 483 years, "Messiah shall be cut off" (Daniel 9:26). These years are each 360 days, i.e. a 'time', so 483 years = 483x360 days = 173880 days = 173880/365.2422 = 476 solar years, approximately. The start year 444 BC is astronomical year -443; so the end year is (-443) + 476 Gregorian years = 33 AD. Now in the interval -443 to 33 the first leap year is -440, and the last leap year is 32, hence there are [32 - (-440)]/ 4 + 1 = 472/4 + 1 = 119 multiples of 4. Three of these multiples, the astronomical centuries -300, -200 and -100, are not however divisible by 400, so 476 Gregorian years = 476x365 days + 116 leap days = 173856 days. Now 173880 days = 173856 days + 24 days, i.e. 476 Gregorian years + 24 days. Hence the date of "Messiah the Prince" is thus:

Saturday 4th March 444 BC + 476 Gregorian years + 24 days = **Saturday 28th March 33 AD**. The significance of this "Messiah the Prince" date is that Saturday 28th March 33 AD, corresponded to 'the tenth' day of the month Abib. (See the chart in the Appendix – Astronomical Dating). On that day the congregation of Israel took for themselves a lamb, which was to be killed four days later.

*Speak to all the congregation of Israel, saying: "**On the tenth [day] of this month every man shall take for himself a lamb**, according to the house of [his] father, a lamb for a household… Now you shall **keep it until the fourteenth day** of the same* *month. Then the whole assembly of the congregation of Israel shall **kill it at twilight**." (Exodus 12:3, 6)*

This was fulfilled by Jesus when he made his triumphal approach to Jerusalem on Saturday 10th Abib (Matthew 21:2-11; John 12:12-19; Mark 11:1-10; Luke 19:29-40). The multitude accepted Jesus as their "Messiah the Prince". They shouted, "Blessed is the King who comes in the name of the Lord" (and so shall He be greeted when He comes again, Matthew 23:39). However four days later, on "the fourteenth day of the same month", i.e. on Wednesday 1st April 33 AD, as the Passover lambs were being killed at twilight, the Messiah was also killed. He was "cut off" (Daniel 9:26). Wednesday means the "fourth day", and in the week of creation the fourth day had seen the giving of light to the earth from the sun and the moon (Genesis 1:14-19). How poignant then, that Wednesday was chosen as the day when the true Light of the world was cut off.

*Then Jesus spoke to them again, saying, "**I am the light of the world**. He who follows Me shall not walk in darkness, but have the light of life." (John 8:12)*

*All things were made through Him, and without Him nothing was made that was made. In Him was life, and the life was the **light** of men… And the **light** shines in the darkness, and the darkness did not comprehend it… That was the **true light** which gives light to every man coming into the world. (John 1:3-5, 9)*

Hence Jesus was crucified on Wednesday 1st April (14th Abib) 33 AD, and He was buried the same day at sunset. He rose from the dead three days later on Saturday 4th April (17th Abib) 33 AD also at sunset.

The visits to the tomb

The visits to the tomb

In what follows, we attempt to harmonise the various visits which were made to the empty tomb (see *The Life of Christ in Stereo*, by Dr. Cheney, J. M. (1969) Portland, Western Baptist Seminary Press. p204-207). The burial of Jesus was followed by three daytimes: The Passover Sabbath on Thursday, the preparation for the weekly Sabbath on Friday, and the weekly Sabbath on Saturday. On Friday daytime, after the *Passover* Sabbath (Mark 16:1), yet before the *weekly* Sabbath (Luke 23:56), the women bought and prepared spices and fragrant oils with which to anoint the body of Jesus. They probably went to the tomb on that day, but found that the guard had been posted there for the three-day period Thursday-Saturday inclusive.

> *On the next day which followed the Day of Preparation (i.e. on the Passover Sabbath day, on Thursday, probably in the morning), the chief priests and Pharisees gathered together to Pilate, saying, 'Sir, we remember, while He was still alive, how that deceiver said, "After three days I will rise." Therefore* ***command that the tomb be made secure until the third day*** *(Thursday, Friday, Saturday), lest His disciples come by night and steal Him [away], and say to the people, "He has risen from the dead." So the last deception will be worse than the first.' Pilate said to them, "You have a guard; go your way, make [it] as secure as you know how." So they went and made the tomb secure, sealing the stone and setting the guard. (Matthew 27:62-66)*

*Now **when the [Passover] Sabbath** (i.e. Wednesday evening-Thursday evening) **was past**, Mary Magdalene, Mary [the mother] of James, and Salome **bought spices** (on Friday, probably in the morning) that they might come and anoint Him. (Mark 16:1)*

*Then they returned and **prepared spices** and fragrant oils. And **they rested on the [weekly] Sabbath** (i.e. Friday evening-Saturday evening) according to the commandment. (Luke 23:56)*

The harmonisation of the visits to the tomb begins at the end of the weekly Sabbath, late Saturday afternoon towards early evening.

1. Late on the (weekly) Sabbath, at the drawing toward the first (day) of the (seven) Sabbaths/weeks, Mary Magdalene and Mary the mother of James the Less and Joses, came to view the tomb (Matthew 28:1). Their purpose for viewing the tomb late on the Saturday Sabbath was probably to see if the guard would in fact leave. They planned to anoint their Lord at first light on Sunday morning, but this would only be possible if the guard would depart from the tomb on Saturday evening.

2. It is almost sunset; it is quiet; and they are in a cemetery. Then all of a sudden, and completely without warning, there is an earthquake (Matthew 28:2). Most probably the women's immediate response would have been to run away and seek safety. Meanwhile the appearance of an angel at the tomb causes the guards to faint from fear (Matthew 28:3-4). Some time later the guards wake up and realizing that the tomb is empty, they return to the city (Matthew 28:11-13). However, curiosity gets the better of Mary Magdalene, and she returns early on the first of the weeks, i.e. on Saturday evening, while it is still dark (John 20:1a). She sees the stone has been taken away, and runs to Peter and John (John

20:1b-2). Peter and John run to the tomb and inspect it (John 20:3-10; Luke 24:12). Mary weeps outside the tomb; talks to two angels; and then to Jesus, whom she mistakes for a gardener (John 20:11-15). Jesus reveals Himself, but does not let her *touch* Him because He has not yet ascended to the Father (John 20:16-17a). Mary tells the disciples that she has seen the Lord, but they do not believe her (John 20:18; Mark 16:9-11).

Jesus ascended to the Father early on the first (day) of the (seven) weeks, i.e. 18th Abib, between Saturday evening 4th April to early Sunday morning 5th April while it was still dark (John 20:1a; 20:17b); Christ was accepted on our behalf as the firstfruit of the spiritual harvest (Colossians 1:18; Revelation 1:5), in fulfilment of the sheaf wave offering (Leviticus 23:10-11); He was glorified (John 7:39); and He returned with the Holy Spirit (John 14:16-20).

3. At first light on Sunday morning, Mary the mother of James, together with Salome, Joanna, and other women, arrive at the tomb bearing spices (Mark 16:2; Luke 24:1). They question, 'who shall move the stone', and are surprised to find it removed (Mark 16:3-4; Luke 24:2). They enter the tomb; do not find the body of Jesus (Mark 16:5a; Luke 24:3); but see a young man sitting on the right side and are amazed (Mark 16:5b).

4. As they are perplexed about this, behold two men stood by them (Luke 24:4). The women were afraid and looked to the ground (Luke 24:5a). They spoke, 'Do not fear; do not be amazed. For I know that you seek Jesus of Nazareth, who was crucified. Why seek the living among the dead? (Matthew 28:5; Mark 16:6a; Luke 24:5b). He is not here, for He has risen, as He said (Matthew 28:6a; Mark 16:6b; Luke 24:6a). Remember how He spoke to you, while He was yet in Galilee, saying "The Son of Man must be delivered into the hands of sinful men, and be crucified, and the third day rise

again'" (Luke 24:6b-7). And they remembered His words (Luke 24:8).

5. 'Come, see the place where they laid Him, where the Lord lay (Mark 16:6c; Matthew 28:6b). But go quickly and tell His disciples, and Peter, that He has risen from the dead, and behold, He is going before you into Galilee; there shall you see Him, as He said to You, lo, I have told you' (Matthew 28:7; Mark 16:7).

6. So they went out quickly and fled from the tomb, with great fear and great joy; and trembling and amazement had seized them (Matthew 28:8a; Mark 16:8a). To no one said they anything, for they were afraid (Mark 16:8b); and they ran to tell His disciples (Matthew 28:8b).

7. And as they went to tell His disciples, behold, Jesus met them, saying, "Rejoice!" So they came and held Him by the feet, and worshipped Him. Then Jesus said to them, "Do not be afraid; go tell my brethren to go into Galilee, and there shall they see Me" (Matthew 28:9-10).

8. And they returned from the tomb and told **all these things** to the eleven, and to the rest. But these words seemed to the apostles as idle tales, and they did not believe them (Luke 24:9, 11).

Jesus appeared to the disciples late on the first day of the weeks during the twilight period of Sunday (18th Abib) 5th April (John 20:1, 19). Not having understood from Scripture that Jesus was to rise again (John 20:9), the disciples' unbelief was only removed when they saw their risen Lord (John 20:20; 1 Corinthians 15:5). At that time the disciples and Peter believed in His resurrection (1 Corinthians 15:1-4; Acts 4:2, 33). In response to their belief Jesus breathed on them and they received the Holy Spirit. (John 20:22)

*Then, the same day at evening, being the first [day] of the week... Jesus came and stood in the midst, and said to them, "Peace [be] with you." When He had said this, He showed them [His] hands and His side. Then the disciples were glad when they saw the Lord. So Jesus said to them again, "Peace to you! As the Father has sent Me, I also send you." And when He had said this, He breathed on [them], and said to them, "**Receive the Holy Spirit**". (John 20:19-22)*

*But you are not in the flesh but in the Spirit, if indeed the **Spirit of God dwells in you**. Now if anyone does not have the Spirit of Christ, he is not His. (Romans 8:9)*

*Not only [that], but we also who have the **firstfruits of the Spirit**, even we ourselves groan within ourselves, eagerly waiting for the adoption, the redemption of our body. (Romans 8:23)*

Problematic verses

Problematic verses

Traditional beliefs have also affected the translation and subsequent interpretation of some verses in the Bible. Two areas which sometimes raise queries are the timing of the Lord's Supper and a time reference which was made by two disciples on the road to Emmaus.

1) Was the Lord's Supper the Passover meal?

The event known as the Lord's Supper was the last meal that Jesus had with His disciples on the evening before the crucifixion. The question we pose here, is whether that meal was the Feast of Unleavened Bread on the 15th Abib at which the Passover lamb was eaten?

One implication of the 14th Abib as the date of the crucifixion, is that the Lord's Supper could not have been the Passover meal. Scripture substantiates that the Lord's Supper was indeed not the Passover meal, by stating that the Lord's Supper occurred "before the feast of the Passover" and by implying that the Feast of the Passover occurred after the crucifixion.

*Now **before the feast of the Passover**, when Jesus knew that His hour had come that He should depart from this world to the Father, having loved His own who were in the world, He loved them to the end. And **supper being ended**, the devil having already put it into the heart of Judas Iscariot, Simon's [son], to betray Him. (John 13:1-2)*

*Then they led Jesus from Caiaphas to the Praetorium, and it was early morning (on the 14th Abib) But they themselves did not go into the Praetorium, lest they should be defiled, but **that they might eat the Passover** (on the following night of the 15th Abib). (John 18:28)*

The main reason why the Lord's Supper has sometimes been associated with the Passover meal, is because of the following verse:

*And He said, "Go into the city to a certain man, and say to him, 'The Teacher says, "My time is at hand; I will **keep** [Gr. Poieo] the Passover at your house with My disciples."'" (Matthew 26:18)*

The Greek word *poieo* is best translated as 'make' and not 'keep'. Some Bible versions have not even attempted to translate *poieo*, but have instead used words to fit the assumed context. Hence the *New International Version (NIV)* renders this verse as, "…I am going to **celebrate** the Passover…"; and *The Living Bible (TLB)* renders it as, "…I will **eat** the Passover…" The above verse however, pertains to making (preparing) the Passover, and not to keeping (eating or celebrating) it. Since Jesus is our Passover "Lamb of God" (John 1:29) "who was sacrificed for us" (1 Corinthians 5:7), could it be that the Passover being prepared was Himself? Two other verses which are mistranslated by both the *Authorised Version (AV)* and the *American Standard Version (ASV)*, are Mark 14:14 and Luke 22:11.

*"Wherever he goes in, say to the master of the house, 'The Teacher says, "Where is the guest room in which I **may** eat [Gr. phago] the Passover with my disciples?"'" (Mark 14:14)*

*"Then you shall say to the master of the house, 'The Teacher says to you, "Where is the guest room in which I **may** eat [Gr. Phago] the Passover with My disciples?"'" (Luke 22:11)*

Here also, because a question was being asked, it is more appropriate to translate *phago* as 'may eat' rather than as 'will eat' or 'shall eat'. Jesus was always very specific with His words, and as happened on other occasion's inferences were not to be implied other than what was explicitly said. The rumour that the apostle John would not die is a good example here.

*Then Peter, turning around, saw the disciple whom Jesus loved following, who also had leaned on His breast at the supper, and said, 'Lord, who is the one who betrays You?' Peter seeing him, said to Jesus, 'But Lord, what [about] this man?' Jesus said to him, "If I will that he remain till I come, what [is that] to you? You follow Me." Then this saying went out among the brethren that this disciple would not die. **Yet Jesus did not say to him that he would not die, but, "If I will that he remain till I come what [is that] to you?"** (John 21:20-23)*

Hence these two verses do not say that Jesus would, or did, eat the Passover, Luke 22:15 also needs explanation. It says, "With desire I have desired to eat this Passover with you before I suffer." Firstly it states 'this' Passover, and not 'the' Passover; and if we consider verses 16-20, it would seem that 'this' Passover, referred to the symbolic act of the giving of His body and the shedding of His blood, which He performed by the breaking and eating of bread, and the sharing and drinking of wine.

*Then He said to them, "With [fervent] desire I have desired to **eat this Passover** with you before I suffer; for I say to you, I will no longer eat of it until it is fulfilled in the kingdom of God".*

*Then He took the cup, and gave thanks, and said, "Take this and divide [it] among yourselves; for I say to you, I will not drink of the fruit of the vine until the kingdom of God comes." And He took bread, gave thanks and broke [it], and gave [it] to them, saying, "**This is My body which is given for you**; do this in remembrance of Me." Likewise He also [took] the cup after supper saying, '**This cup [is] the new covenant in My blood, which is shed for you**." (Luke 22:15-20)*

2) The disciples on the road to Emmaus

Luke 24:13-27 tells the story of when Jesus met two disciples on the road to Emmaus.

*Now on the first [day] of the week...two of them were traveling that same day to a village called Emmaus... And they talked together of **all these things which had happened**... So it was, while they conversed and reasoned, that Jesus Himself drew near and went with them...And He said to them, "What kind of conversation [is] this that you have with one another...?" Cleopas answered and said to Him... 'have You not known the things which happened there in these days?' And He said to them, "What things?" So they said to Him, '**The things concerning Jesus of Nazareth**, who was a Prophet mighty in deed and word before God and all the people, and how the chief priests and our rulers **delivered Him to be condemned to death, and crucified Him**. But we were hoping that it was He who was going to redeem Israel. Indeed, besides all this, **today is the third day since these things happened**.' (Luke 24:1, 13-21)*

Jesus was crucified on Wednesday the 14th Abib, but the tomb was sealed and guarded on Thursday the 15th Abib, on the Sabbath 'high day'. The disciples met Jesus "on the first of the weeks" (Luke 24:1), i.e. the 18th Abib, sometime between Saturday evening and Sunday evening. Since the evening was approaching (Luke 24:29) their meeting with Jesus probably took place during Sunday afternoon The problem verse here is Luke 24:21, which says that it was the "third day since these things happened". However, for Sunday to have been the "third day since these things happened.", the details of "these things" would have had to include the Thursday sealing and guarding of the tomb. The phrase "all these things" was first used in Luke 24:9, in reference to the report from the women that they had found the tomb empty. That was the latest "thing" which had happened, and they knew about it because they mentioned it to Jesus in Luke 24:22-24.

*Then they returned from the tomb and told **all these things** to the eleven and **to all the rest**. (Luke 24:9)*

*"Yes, and **certain women** of our company, who arrived at the tomb early, astonished us. When they **did not find His body**, they came saying that they had also seen a vision of angels who said He was alive. And **certain of those [who were] with us went to the tomb and found [it] just as the women had said**; but Him they did not see." (Luke 24:22-24)*

The narrative does not mention explicitly that the disciples talked about the sealing of the tombstone or the setting of the guard (Matthew 27:62-66), but considering the importance of these two measures to prevent Jesus rising again, it does deem very probable that they were included in their talking "together of all these things which had happened" (Luke 24:14). The conversation the disciples had with Jesus must have included more words than were recorded in verses 15-31. For instance their statement in verse 21 that it was the "third day since these things happened" is without context, unless it had been mentioned previously. As a conjecture we suspect the order of their conversation went something like this:

1) They first talked about the latest known thing, i.e. the report from the women, Peter and John that the tomb was found empty.

2) They would then have talked about the guard having been posted at the tomb on the Thursday and queried whether the absence of the guard had anything to do with the absence of the body of Jesus

3) Then they met Jesus, and not knowing who He was, had to backtrack the story to who Jesus was, and about His life and crucifixion.

Hence points 1 to 3 included "all the things" about which they conversed. It is probable that they associated the events of the burial and the posting of the guard as one event, namely the entombment of Jesus. Hence the only time span that leaves between "all the things" they talked about was the three days between points 1 and 2. Why should we assume that the disciples knew that the three days commenced from the time of Christ's burial? If they had understood that, then why were there only women and guards anywhere near the tomb when Jesus was resurrected? We contend that there was still ambiguity concerning the correct start and end time of the three days. This ambiguity has persisted for 2000 years, only now we somehow manage to assign a mere 36 hours to three days. In fact it is even worse than that, for if Jesus was indeed resurrected at 6 pm on Saturday then a burial on Friday at 6 pm would only involve an interval of 24 hours!

Summary remarks

Summary remarks

Jesus came to fulfil the Law and the Prophets (Matthew 5:17). Hence a faithful study of the death and resurrection of Jesus must include the fact that it was the time of Passover, i.e. it must address the relevance of the day of Unleavened Bread; the killing of the Passover lamb; the Feast of Unleavened Bread (a Sabbath day on which the Passover lamb was eaten); the days of offering made by fire and the eating of unleavened bread; the sheaf wave offering (as directed by the rulership of the Sadducees, i.e. the day after the weekly Sabbath following Passover); the seven weeks; and the Feast of weeks (Pentecost). Much of what has been written may be considered controversial, and anyone with the means is urged to further this investigation in the following area: Despite orthodox Jews' rejection of Jesus as their long awaited Messiah, what *day-date-year,* and *time*, do they hold that the historical person of Jesus was crucified?

Jesus was buried at sunset at the end of a Jewish daytime, which is from sunrise to sunset. Hence no part of 14th Abib can be counted as the time Jesus spent in the tomb. We contend that the belief of a Good Friday Resurrection and Sunday morning resurrection just does not hold. For in such a case only 15th Abib (Friday evening to Saturday evening) and part of 16th Abib (Saturday evening to Sunday morning) could be considered as burial time. But that only involves part of two calendar days, and not part of three days as has been assumed. Hence even the argument of counting parts of three days as a whole does not hold by Jewish time reckoning. We conclude that Jesus was crucified on Wednesday 1st April 33 AD. He was buried the same day at sunset, and He rose from the dead exactly 3 days later on Saturday 4th April 33 AD also at sunset.

The days of unleavened bread

The days of unleavened bread

Time	1800	2100	2400	0300	0600	0900	1200	1500	1800
Jewish hr	-	-	-	-	3rd	6th	9th	12th
	Evening			:		Morning			
Date				:					

14 Abib	1st day of Unleavened Bread/Leaven removed/Passover killed at twilight

	1	2	:		3	4	← 5 →6	7

(Tuesday)   : (Wednesday)

15 Abib	**1st day eat unleavened bread** Sabbath/Feast of Unleavened Bread/Passover eaten

	8	:		9		

(Wednesday)   : (Thursday)

16 Abib	2nd day eat unleavened bread/Preparation day of the weekly Sabbath

	:		10		

(Thursday)   : (Friday)

17 Abib	**Weekly Sabbath**/3rd day eat unleavened bread

	:			11

(Friday)   : (Saturday)

18 Abib	4th day eat unleavened bread/1st day of the seven weeks/Sheaf wave offering

	12	:			13

(Saturday)   : (Sunday)

19 Abib	5th day eat unleavened bread/2nd day of the weeks

:

(Sunday)   : (Monday)

20 Abib	6th day eat unleavened bread/3rd day of the weeks

:

(Monday)   : (Tuesday)

21 Abib	**7th day eat unleavened bread Sabbath**/4th day of the weeks

:

(Tuesday)   : (Wednesday)

Events

1 Prepare for Passover (Mt 26:17-19; Mk 14:12-16; Lk 22:7-13).

2 Lord's Supper (Mt 26:20-29; Mk 14:17-25; Lk 22:14-20). It was the evening period (after 6 pm) at the start of the first day of Unleavened Bread. It was not yet time to start eating unleavened bread, which began from the twilight period at the end of the 14th Abib. It was not the Passover meal (Jn 13:1-2; 18:28).

3 *Christ Condemned* by both Jews and Romans (Mt 27:1-3; Jn 19:13-16).

4 *Christ Crucified* (Mk 15:25) on the Preparation Day of the annual Passover Sabbath (Jn 19:31,14a).

5 Darkness (Mt 27:45; Mk 15:33; Lk 23:44).

6 *Christ Died* (Mt 27:46-50; Mk 15:34-37). The time coincided with the killing of the Passover lamb (Ex 12:6; Dt 16:6).

7 *Christ Buried* (Mt 27:57-60; Mk 15:42-46; Lk 23:50-54; Jn 19:38-42).

8 Passover eaten (Ex 12:8-10).

9 Tomb sealed and guarded (time uncertain) (Mt 27:62-66).

10 Spices bought=purchased (not brought) after (high) Sabbath (Mk 16:1) and prepared before (weekly) Sabbath (Lk 23:56) (times uncertain). It indicates two Sabbaths.

11 *Christ Risen* (Mt 12:38-40; 16:21; 28:1-6; Mk 8:31; Jn 2:19).

12 *Christ Ascended to the Father* (Jn 20:17b); Christ was accepted on our behalf as the firstfruit of the spiritual harvest (Colossians 1:18; Revelation 1:5), in fulfilment of the sheaf wave offering (Leviticus 23:10-11); He was glorified (Jn 7:39); and He returned with the Spirit (John 14:16-20). (Time uncertain)

13 The disciples and Peter believed His resurrection (1 Cor 15:1-5; Jn 20:8-9,19-21).

The days
of the seven
Sabbaths/weeks

The days of the seven Sabbaths/weeks

The days of the 'seven weeks/Sabbaths' (Leviticus 23:15; Deuteronomy 16:9):

Night Day	wk1	wk2	wk3	wk4	wk5	wk6	wk7	
Sat - Sun	1	8	15	22	29	36	43	(50)
Sun - Mon	2	9	16	23	30	37	44	
Mon - Tues	3	10	17	24	31	38	45	
Tues - Wed	4	11	18	25	32	39	46	
Wed - Thu	5	12	19	26	33	(40)	47	
Thu - Fri	6	13	20	27	34	41	48	
Fri - Sat	7.	14.	21.	28.	35.	42.	49. -7Sabbaths	

We have demonstrated previously that the crucifixion of our Lord occurred during the daytime of Wednesday 14th Abib 33 AD. Hence the next weekly Sabbath on Friday evening-Saturday evening occurred on the 17th Abib 33 AD. The first day of the seven Sabbaths/weeks was the day after that weekly Sabbath, i.e. Saturday evening-Sunday evening the 18th Abib. On that day the high priest on earth waved a sheaf before God in heaven in thanks-giving of the firstfruits of the barley harvest. And at that same time Christ ascended to heaven and was accepted on our behalf as the firstfruit of the spiritual harvest (Colossians 1:18; Revelation 1:5), in fulfilment of the sheaf wave offering. (Leviticus 23:10-11)

*Speak to the children of Israel, and say to them: "When you come into the land which I give to you, and reap its harvest, then you shall **bring a sheaf of the firstfruits of your harvest to the priest**. He shall wave the sheaf before the LORD, to be accepted on your behalf; **on the day after the Sabbath the priest shall wave it**." (Leviticus 23:10-11)*

*Jesus said to her, "Do not cling to Me, for I have not yet ascended to My Father; but go to My brethren and say to them, '**I am ascending to My Father** and your Father, and [to] My God and your God.'" (John 20:17)*

The 4th day of the Sabbaths was Tuesday evening-Wednesday evening the 21st Abib. That day was the seventh day of eating unleavened bread (Leviticus 23:6) and of making offerings by fire to the Lord (Leviticus 23:8a). It was a Sabbath day of holy gathering (Leviticus 23:8b). Jesus was first seen alive on the first day of the weeks, and He was 'taken/carried up' into heaven on the 40th day.

*The former account I made, O Theophilus, of all that Jesus began to do and teach, until the day in which He was taken up, after He through the Holy Spirit had given commandments to the apostles whom He had chosen, to whom He also presented Himself alive after His suffering by many infallible proofs, **being seen by them during forty days** and speaking of the things pertaining to the kingdom of God ... Now when He had spoken these things, while they watched, **He was taken up**, and a cloud received Him out of their sight. (Acts 1:1-3, 9)*

*And He led them out as far as Bethany, and He lifted up His hands and blessed them. Now it came to pass, while He blessed them, that **He was parted from them and carried up into heaven**. (Luke 24:50-51)*

Now the Jewish month Abib has 30 days, and it is followed by the Jewish months of Zif and Sivan which have 29 days and 30 days respectively. Hence the 40th day of the Sabbaths/weeks, the day Jesus was taken up into heaven, was Wednesday evening-Thursday evening 27th Zif 33 AD, i.e. 13-14 May 33 AD.

The Feast of Weeks (Pentecost)

The Feast of Weeks (Pentecost)

The day after the seven Sabbaths, i.e. the 50th (Pentecost), was the 'Feast of Weeks' (Deuteronomy 16:10-12). Pentecost was on Saturday evening-Sunday evening, 8th Sivan 33 AD, i.e. 23-24 May 33 AD. On that day new grain flour was baked with leaven (filling) and waved to the Lord as a new grain offering.

> Count **fifty days to the day after the seventh Sabbath**; then you shall offer a **new grain offering** to the LORD. You shall bring from your dwellings **two wave [loaves]**of two-tenths [of an ephah]. They shall be of fine flour; they shall be **baked with leaven**. **[They are] the firstfruits to the Lord**. And you shall offer with the bread seven lambs of the first year, without blemish, one young bull, and two rams. They shall be [as] a burnt offering to the LORD, with their grain offering and their drink offerings, an offering made by fire for a sweet aroma to the LORD. Then you shall sacrifice one kid of the goats as a sin offering, and two male lambs of the first year as a sacrifice of a peace offering. The priest shall **wave them with the bread of the firstfruits [as]a wave offering** before the LORD, with the two lambs. They shall be holy to the LORD for the priest. And you shall proclaim on the same day [that] it is a holy convocation to you. You shall do no customary work [on it. It shall be] a statute forever in all your dwellings throughout your generations. (Leviticus 23:16-21)

On that same day, namely Sunday 24 May 33 AD, Jesus sent the promise of the Father-the baptism in the Holy Spirit *into witnessing in power* through being filled with the Holy Spirit. (Acts 2:1-41)

*Behold, I send the **Promise of My Father** upon you; but tarry in the city of Jerusalem until you are **endued with power** from on high. (Luke 24:49)*

*Nevertheless I tell you the truth. It is to your advantage that I go away; for if I do not go away, the Helper will not come to you; **but if I depart, I will send Him to you**. (John 16:7)*

*And being assembled together with [them], He commanded them not to depart from Jerusalem, but to wait for the **Promise of the Father**, "which", [He said], "you have heard from Me; for John truly baptised with water but you shall be **baptised with the Holy Spirit** not many days from now... But you shall **receive power when the Holy Spirit has come upon you**; and shall **be witnesses to Me** in Jerusalem, and in all Judea and Samaria, and to the end of the earth." (Acts 1:4-5, 8)*

*Now when the **Day of Pentecost had fully come**, they were all with one accord in one place. And suddenly there came **a sound from heaven**, as of a rushing mighty wind, and it **filled the whole house** where they were sitting. Then there appeared to them divided tongues, as of fire, and [one] sat upon each of them. And they were **all filled with the Holy Spirit** and began to speak with other tongues, as the Spirit gave them utterance... But this is what was spoken by the prophet Joel: "And it shall come to pass in the last days", says God, "that **I will pour out of My Spirit on all flesh**; your sons and your daughters shall prophesy, your young men shall see visions, your old men shall dream dreams. And on My menservants and on My maidservants I will pour out My Spirit in those days; and they shall prophesy"... This Jesus God has raised up, of which we are all witnesses. Therefore being exalted to the right hand of God, and having received from the Father **the promise of the Holy Spirit**, He poured out this which you now see and hear...*

For **the promise is to you and to your children**, and to all who are afar off, as many as the Lord our God will call. *(Acts 2:1-4, 16-18, 32-34, 39)*

Appendix 1. History of the Jewish lunar calendar

Appendix 1. History of the Jewish lunar calendar

The calendar systems used by Israel throughout their history was influenced by that of their neighbouring nations. All the ancient Near Eastern countries based their calendars on the lunar cycle. Alone in the ancient world the Egyptians had a calendar based on a solar year of 365 days, divided into three seasons of four months, each having 30 days, i.e.

$$3 \times 4 \times 30 = 360 \text{ days.}$$

The 5 'additional days' not included in the number of months were added at the end of every year. This calendar was used by the Jews before the Exodus, as recorded by Moses. The Egyptian solar year is approximately 0.24220 days shorter than the true solar year. (The effect of the error would have accumulated each year. For instance, after a 2520 year period the error would have been

$$2520 \times 0.24220 = 610 \text{ days approximately).}$$

After the Exodus, Jewish months began with the observing of the appearance of New Moons (1 Chronicles 23:31; 2 Chronicles 2:4). New Moons are at intervals of approximately 29.5 days, hence the Jewish year was

$$12 \times 29.5 = 354 \text{ days.}$$

This lunar year is approximately 11 days shorter than the true solar year. The first month of the sacred year (Exodus 12:2) was Abib (Mar-Apr); whereas the Civil year commenced at the New Moon of Tisri (Sep-Oct). No exact information is available to explain how the Jews originally adjusted their inaccurate lunar calendar to synchronise with the actual solar year. (To make up the difference they probably used the practice of insertion, known as intercalation: periodically adding an extra intercalary month whenever the discrepancy between the solar year and their lunar year became too noticeable). In Babylon, by the 6th Century BC, an additional month called Adaru was added at fixed three-yearly intervals. There were three leap years within a recurring 8-year cycle. (Assuming accurate observation of New Moons at approximately 29.5-day intervals, after each 8-year period the error was

$$8 \times 365.24220 - 8 \times 354 - 3 \times 29.5 = 1.4376 \text{ days}).$$

The Persian Empire took over this system and in this way it was passed on to the Jews. (The beginning of each new month was proclaimed by the Sanhedrin on the basis of the evidence of two eyewitnesses to the appearance of the New Moon at dusk. The news was announced by beacon-fires kindled in sequence round the country or, later on, by messengers). It had been known since the 5th century BC, that 235 (= 19 x 12 + 7) True lunations/synodic months (29.5305-day months) or 19 True lunar years (354.3671-day years) + 7 synodic months, contain exactly the same number of days as 19 solar years. This was discovered by the Greek astronomer Meton in 433 BC, and is known as the Metonic Cycle. From the 7th century BC until the reign of Julius Caesar, the Roman year was composed of 12 lunar months of 29 and 30 days alternating. Fixing the length of the months removed the need to observe New Moons. It was still a

$$6 \times 30 + 6 \times 29 = 354 \text{ - day year.}$$

The Roman calendar was modified by Julius Caesar in 46 BC to a year of 365.25 days. In the time of our Lord Jesus, despite the rulership of Rome over Israel they maintained their own calendar. Hence the Jewish calendar in use at that time was probably one composed of 12 lunar months of 29 and 30 days alternating, with a 30-day intercalary month every 3 years. (Hence after each 8-year period the error was

$$8 \times 365.24220 - 8 \times 354 - 3 \times 30$$
$$= -0.0624 \text{ days} = -1.5 \text{ hours approximately).}$$

Late in Israel's history the Jewish Civil calendar was probably officially introduced by the patriarch Hillel II in AD 338. It was composed of 12 lunar months of 29 and 30 days alternating. An extra 30-day month was inserted between the months Adar and Nisan, in order to celebrate the agricultural festivals in their proper season. That month, sometimes called Veadar ('22nd Adar'), was added seven times within a 19-year cycle, in years 3, 6, 8/9, 11, 14, 17, 19. (After each 19-year period the error was

$$19 \times 365.24220 - 19 \times 354 - 7 \times 30 = 3.6018 \text{ days).}$$

The beginning of the Civil year may be shifted because of the rule that the Day of Atonement (Tisri 10) must not fall on Friday or Sunday (i.e. immediately before or after the weekly Sabbath); or the 7th day of Tabernacles (Tisri 21) on a weekly Sabbath. (The effect of this is that the day part of Tisri 1 is restricted from falling on Wednesday, Friday or Sunday). Because of this, non-leap years can have 353-355 days, and leap years 383-385 days.

The months of the Jewish Civil calendar:

	Month	Days	
1	Nisan/Abib	30	(Mar-Apr)
2	Zif	29	(Apr-May)
3	Sivan	30	(May-Jun)
4	Tammuz	29	(Jun-Jul)
5	Ab	30	(Jul-Aug)
6	Elul	29	(Aug-Sep)
7	Ethanim/Tisri	30	(Sep-Oct)
8	Marchesvan/Bul	29	(Oct-Nov)
9	Chisleu	30	(Nov-Dec)
10	Tebeth	29	(Dec-Jan)
11	Sebat	30	(Jan-Feb)
12	Adar	29	(Feb-Mar)
		354	*Lunar year*
	Veadar	30	(Intercalary month)
		384	*Lunar leap year*

Appendix 2. Astronomical dating

Appendix 2.
Astronomical dating

The Sun and the Moon are two great astronomical clocks which God set in the heavens, "for signs and seasons, and for days and years" (Genesis 1:14). Hence astronomical identification of New Moons, which are coincident with the beginning of Jewish months, should reveal the Gregorian date of Christ's crucifixion on 14th Abib 33 AD. The following chart details the astronomical date and Jerusalem time of New Moons, and Full Moons or Lunar eclipses, in the year of the crucifixion. It also indicates the probable dates of the Jewish months. (Since the Jewish day is from sunset to sunset, each 'Jewish date' corresponds to 1800-2400 hours of one day of the week, and 0000-1800 hours of the following day of the week). The week 'Day' elating to the 'Time' of New Moons, and Full Moons or Lunar eclipses is underlined:

Moon	Jewish	date	Day	Date	AD	Time
N	Tisri	1	Mon-Tue	Sep 23	32	13:47
LE	Tisri	15	Mon-Tue	Oct 7	32	17:14
N	Bul	1	Wed-Thu	Oct 23	32	06:05
F	Bul	15	Wed-Thu	Nov 6	32	06:19
N	Chisley	2	Fri-Sat	Nov 21	32	20:52
F	Chisley	16	Fri-Sat	Dec 5	32	21:38
N	Tebeth	1	Sat-Sun	Dec 21	32	09:41
F	Tebeth	15	Sat-Sun	Jan 4	33	14:44
N	Sebat	2	Mon-Tue	Jan 19	33	20:42
F	Sebat	16	Mon-Tue	Feb 3	33	08:52
N	Adar	1	Tue-Wed	Feb 18	33	06:22
F	Adar	16	Wed-Thu	Mar 5	33	02:52
N	Abib	1	Wed-Thu	Mar 19	33	15:12
LE	Abib	17	Fri-Sat	Apr 3	33	19:23
N	Zif	1	Fri-Sat	Apr 17	33	23:43
F	Zif	16	Sat-Sun	May 3	33	09:28
N	Sivan	1	Sat-Sun	May 17	33	08:33
F	Sivan	17	Mon-Tue	Jun 1	33	20:53
Key:	N=New Moon;		F=Full Moon;	LE=Lunar	eclipse	

If Abib AD 33 was not preceded by an intercalation, then the New Moon of the month Abib occurred on Thursday 19th March at 3:12 pm. Now, the coming of Jesus into the world was in the fullness of time.

> But **when the fullness of the time had come, God sent forth His Son,** born of a woman, born under the law. (Galatians 4:4)

With similar certainty, the chronological clock was precisely running throughout His life, so the Jewish day 1st Abib would have exactly coincided with the New Moon Hence the 1st Abib predicted by the 8-year lunar calendar in use at that time, most probably occurred on the Jewish day Wednesday evening 18th March to Thursday evening 19th March 33 AD. Consequently, the 14th Abib covered the period Tuesday evening 31st March to Wednesday evening 1st April. Hence Jesus was crucified on Wednesday 1st April 33 AD. He was buried the same day at sunset, and He rose from the dead exactly 3 days later on Saturday 4th April 33 AD also at sunset.

****

About the author

Peter John-Charles was born in 1961 in London. He was educated at St. Bede's School, Bradford, before reading Mathematics at the University of Sheffield. He then undertook research and obtained his PhD in Mathematics from the University of Dundee, Scotland, At present he works in computing and lives in Yorkshire.

****

For a full list of books available from
The Open Bible Trust,
please visit

www.obt.org.uk

Also on Chronology

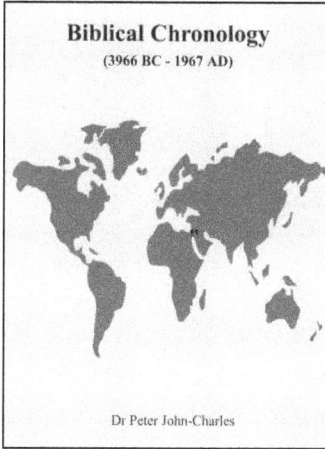

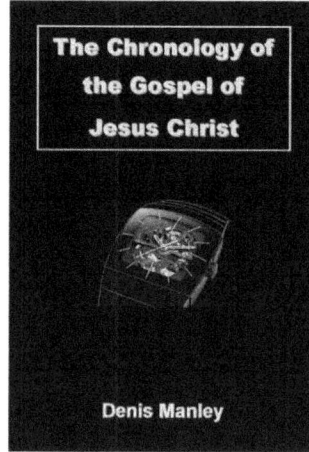

Biblical Chronology
(3966 BC - 1967 AD)

Dr Peter John-Charles

The Chronology of
the Gospel of
Jesus Christ

Denis Manley

Biblical Chronology
Dr Peter John-Charles

The Chronology of the Gospel of Jesus Christ
Denis Manley

Further details of these books can be seen on **www.obt.org.uk**

They can be ordered from that website and also from

The Open Bible Trust
Fordland Mount, Upper Basildon,
Reading, RG8 8LU, UK.

Search magazine

About this book

When was Christ's Death and Resurrection?

Frequently the Eastern Church and the Western Church celebrate Easter on different dates so … when was Christ's death and resurrection?

Some suggest that the significance of these outstanding events far out-weighs any quibbling over times and dates. That may be true, but any such reaction to the title of this publication will quickly be dispelled. Through painstaking application of Scripture, and his good grasp of the Jewish calendar, the author shows that the traditional time-scale of these events to be untenable. He puts forward a different scenario, one which better harmonizes with the biblical record.

However, the great value in these pages is in discovering just how perfectly the Lord Jesus Christ fulfilled the types and shadows contained in the Law and the Prophets. Seemingly dull Levitical ritual bursts into life as we appreciate more fully its wondrous significance in pointing to Israel's Messiah. Sadly, the traditional time-table hides much of this edifying truth - truth confirmation the great work of redemption accomplished by our Lord Jesus Christ.

Those who read this study will find it a valuable faith building exercise.

Publications of The Open Bible Trust must be in accordance with its evangelical, fundamental and dispensational basis. However, beyond this minimum, writers are free to express whatever beliefs they may have as their own understanding, provided that the aim in so doing is to further the object of The Open Bible Trust. A copy of the doctrinal basis is available at

www.obt.org.uk/doctrinal-basis

or from:

THE OPEN BIBLE TRUST
Fordland Mount, Upper Basildon,
Reading, RG8 8LU, GB

www.ingramcontent.com/pod-product-compliance
Lightning Source LLC
Chambersburg PA
CBHW061753020426
42331CB00006B/1464